EVEN GOD

HAD TO DIE

ARKOPAUL DAS

FOR YA'LL

OTHER BOOKS BY ARKOPAUL
DAS

THE DEAD VETERAN

INSOMNIAC

LIMOUSINE

LIVE ON THE EDGE

SOCIOPATH: DECEITFUL GAME

YOU NEED TO HEAR THIS SHIT

BLOG :
thoughtsadora.blogspot.com

"You can't run away from your problems if you are dehydrated. You can, but you won't get very far."

- Pete Davidson.

The air begins to feel a little heavy,
As the shadows looms over your head,
The lights go off the buildings slow and
steady,
You realise the pile of mess you have made.
And you'll fall, to walk again,
But this nightmare, it never ends,
The streets go quiet, here comes the rain,
Of sorrow, regret and amends.
And the loneliness creeps up on you,
Asks you about the time you spent -
With yourself; who was never new,
And those times that you now resent.
And you fall to walk again,
The clouds gather, the darkness never ends,
The struggle you went through, goes in vain,
Waiting for a helping hand that no one
sends.
The air begins to feel a little clear,
As the light pours in from the blinds.
The demons of hell are nowhere near,
Until sun sets and they step out of your
mind.
And you'll fall, all over again,
It will eat you up, all the same,

Arkopaul Das

Wanting to give up, this constant pain,
Make it stop in god's name.

Sometimes I walk into a situation and get
caught off guard,
A familiar scent or a scarf dissolving in the
distance,
Takes me back to the what once was,
To those fleeting glimpses of that love,
Or those silly laughter that would surround
the room,
For what once was.
The special stash in my memories is now
yellow and wrinkly,
The letters reminiscing poetry, lyrics and
words,
Are now erased with work and
responsibilities,
Those long conversations till the sun sets,
And those long walks in a warm summer
day,
Fleeting moments of deja vu used to flood
my veins,
Whenever I dared to open the doors to my
nostalgia ridden heart,
And I cling to it; to everything that's still
sweet and innocent,
The childish giggles and a glint of reflection

Arkopaul Das

from the afternoon sun,
Those familiar melodies floating from the
nearby stereo,
And a uproar in my novice heart,
Screaming the happiness out loud,
I cling to it because I'll never have that
again,
Cos I will always crave for,
what once was.

X--X

Every time she sees them smile,
Playing around like tiny angels from heaven,
She feels a punch of regret.
A dark treacherous abyss opens up within
her,
A sense of compunction creeps up behind
her spine -
and felicitates a row of shivers,
Cos who was she to play the executioner?
She sees the blurred shadows at night,
When she's alone and the door creeps open,
And a silhouette walks in with a smile,
Peering down at her with gauged out eyes,
Asking her with a shrill voice " Why did you
do it, why?"
She jolts back awake weeping to notice
the shadow retreating back in the distance.
Back inside her mind, engraving the guilt,
in her memory.
Realizing what day it was,
She blew the candles on the cake like every
year,
With tears in her eyes
And guilt in her heart, yet again,

She whispered to the gloomy room, "Happy birthday. Today you'd have been seven"

X--X

Arkopaul Das

Back in the day, when we were young,
We would play a game called hide and seek.
I was never the one to close my eyes
and count to ten.
I was always the one to run away and
squeeze myself,
In the smallest space available,
And crouch there uncomfortably, waiting to
be found.
I realized even now, we are all doing it,
Every moment, every second of the day.
We are all running away from our fears,
from attachments, from our loved ones,
from our ambitions, passions,
Closing off our eyes and ears, and ignoring
the people
calling our names.
I could never be the one to find people,
I never felt like it would be worth it.
I never tried to look for the people hiding,
Cos I felt like they were sitting there
comfortably,
While I was the one putting all the effort.
But now that I'm on the other side of the

tide,
Waiting and waiting, to be found,
To be held and to be understood,
To be loved and cared for,
To finally break down all the barriers and
give in,
I realized I want to be the one who puts
himself out there,
Find the ones who need nurturing,
Fill their veins with my own ecstasy,
And make the world a better place.

X——X

Someday I want to feel alive.
I wanna wake up with a smile with
the sun shinning down on my face,
I want to be able to run to work,
Clutching my latte in one hand.
I want to spend my time writing,
Surrounding myself with books,
Sense of adventure and thrill,
Love and poetry,
Flowing through my veins.
Someday I wanna feel alive.
I wanna get down on my knees,
And put a ring on my love,
I want to venture into the unknown,
Discover places I can't even pronounce,
And take the road not taken often.
Cos someday I wanna feel alive.
I wanna work hard, and feel healthy,
Satisfied and productive,
I want to make daring mistakes,
And be spontaneous,
I want to sit back and relax, and
go paragliding at the same time.
Cos someday I wanna feel alive.
I wanna grow old and relax on the beach,

EVEN GOD HAD TO DIE

While I see my kids run away from the
waves,
I wanna see the sky turn crimson,
And watch the sun go down below the
horizon,
With a smile pasted on my face,
Knowing that I have lived my life,
To the fullest.
Cos someday I wanna feel alive.

Arkopaul Das

Is this a gift or a curse?
The fact that I learnt to look beyond what's
obvious,
At a very early age.
Nothing is as it seems, no one is as they
seem.

That shy girl in your class,
Is probably the most talkative when she's
with her person.
That guy who's always cracking jokes in the
cafeteria,
Is probably the one who's crying his eyes
out at night,
That loner who seems like he doesn't care
about anyone,
Is probably the most caring guy in the
world.
The dad who rudely said he couldn't buy
you something,
Is probably working day and night to
provide food on your plate.
The country that gets bombed and
destroyed,

Is probably the country with the most
peaceful people.

But it doesn't mean everyone is decent.
That guy who has joined the candle march
for justice,
is probably a potential rapist himself.
That politician promising betterment for the
citizens,
Is probably gonna forget about it after you
vote for him.
That girl who seems the most innocent,
Might just be fucking around behind your
back.
That's why shallow small talk doesn't
interest me,
That's why I learnt to look deeper into the
soul of everybody.
And when I really find out who they are, I
wonder,
Is this a gift, or a curse?

x—x

Arkopaul Das

I hit the gas and thought of,
The first day that I met you,
Your beauty was such that,
It filled made me feel alive,
The smile, or the heart,
Or the color of your soul,
I wanted to give you more than my world,
I wanted to make you more than my wife.
As we went out and found our vibe,
It felt like unicorns in a morning sky,
We sang to the clouds, and we danced in the
rain,
Then we had our last supper after midnight.
The magic in your eyes, the touch of your
skin,
The heaven that you showed me, oh where
do I begin?
Days went by, and slowly,
You became a part of me.
Now you lay there, your eyes so sore,
You never told me, you had stage four,
You held my hand, and drifted away,
To go up in flames the very next day.
My car neared the end, and hit it hard,
The flames went up like a wingless bird,

As it crept to my bones and reached my eye,
I began to realize why god had to die.

I saw the sun set, with tears in my eyes,
The darkness came over me like a blessing
in disguise,
There was still more to life, more plans to
devise,
Once I've let go, I don't get enticed, twice.
Dice, I was rolled around like a dice,
Never even noticed that it was you,
Who led me to my demise,
Throttled by your waves I'd rise,
While that felt nice,
You still treated me like a boat, capsized,
Now that the sun has set, let me surmise,
Someone else's name is meant to be written,
In my hearts emblem,
It won't matter if my life darkens,
Cos fuck light I'm all about carpe noctem.
I was one in a million,
I was perfect, you went wrong,
I'll live this good life even when I'm a
wreck,
As I sit here watching the dawn break.

x—x

As blood ran down my arm,
The realization crashed in on me again,
I didn't wanna go,
I looked up as you came down low,
Torch in hand you floated so slow.
You reached down and held out your hand,
Darkness swallowed me up like quicksand,
I whispered, "I plead guilty, take me instead
Whatever you punished her for, send them
all my way"
His grim eyes looked at me and spoke, "If I
wanted her dead, I'd let her live,
You wanted to visit my place, I believe?
But boy don't you see? You've always been
in the grave,
And you shall stay, no matter how much you
crave death "
The darkness disappeared as I thought ;
I'll reach oblivion or maybe not,
But I woke up, as my eyes slowly cleared,
I felt an ache and saw the light,
IVs stuck in me but out of sight, "He is
back! " they sobbed with deep breaths.
And the realization crashed in on me again,
I am alive but this is death.

EVEN GOD HAD TO DIE

There was only a few things that would
dazzle me
at a first glance.
The alluring aura of the flowing hair,
Cascading down her shoulders,
Glistening in the sun kissed afternoon,
Or the hypnotic vibes her dove like eyes
radiate,
Every time she stretches her lips,
And engages in a tantalizing smile;
Which is so vibrant and polychromatic,
It could render a rainbow to grey.
A touch of inveigled mischief adorning
those dimples,
With a strand of loose hair slithering down
her forehead,
Occasionally getting towed back behind the
ear,
Assorted with a soft genial voice;
igniting psychedelic explosions in me.
Or is it the enticing vibes she unfurls
with her mesmerizing mannerisms,
Accompanied with a luscious gleam in her
eyes, that occurred,
When she opened her mouth to utter those

words,
And the brim of her lips grazed my earlobe,
Amorously filling my veins with the
fragrance of intimacy,
And bewitch me with not only her beauty,
But with her inner artistic elegance,
incapacitating me of any further
undertaking.
She isn't just a trip you take when you are
stultified with life,
She is an expedition that you take till the
end of earth.

Sitting there, star lit skies,
Eclipsed moon, starry night,
Scribbled thoughts, misty eyes,
Bittersweet memories, heart cries.
Ink on paper, words flow,
Skin on skin, a warm glow,
Hand in hand, time slows,
The illusion disappears as wind blows.
Hate and love, the heart sighs,
Porcelain face, a beautiful disguise,
Nightmares and daydreams, known allies,
Broken inside, emotions die.
Melancholy surrounds, feelings ablate,
Clouds cover the sky, darkness set.
Once a light but now a living briquette,
More days, means more regrets.
Brush of chilly wind, the eclipse ends,
Staunched veins, cracks open,
Bleeds the last words, lies unwoven,
The wolf howls, her blood rains.

x—x

It's not easy to be in touch with your
emotions ,
When you are up and running with your life,
Constabtly keeping a straight face on, and
hide,
From the judgemental glares,
Devoiding yourself of any feelings.
It's never good to remain one dimensional
like a robot,
Like the world expects us to be ,
Always happy and doing what they want,
Because for real, shit builds up inside that
even we don't notice,
No matter how positive you try to be,
The world will always punch your face ,
And give you reasons to give up until you
actually die,
So don't pretend it's all good.
Don't pretend like you have never made
mistakes,
Like you are the victim, cos it happens to
almost everyone.
Sit back and cry if needed,
Take your time to get over certain things

instead of
Denying what you really feel.
Remember sadness is an art,
When sadness flows through your veins you
get to ;
Channel it into something productive,
And bring out that creative side of you,
Which you didn't even know, existed.
Be sad or weak or even vulnerable,When
necessary,
it's normal human reactions
To a fucked up situation and it's really okay,
But once you get over it, get your swag back
on,
And hussle till you are at the top.

X—X

Arkopaul Das

You can try to describe yourself,
And curve your words perfectly,
But you can't you can't deny the fact that,
No one can be poetry.
You wished to be soft spoken, and make
those hearts melt,
You wished even the harshest words would
come out sweetly,
And explain how you felt.
Your skin isn't exquisite, and your jawline
isn't sharp,
You can lie about your features in your
musings,
But you can't take back the emotions that
you faked.
Your life has never been so smooth,
You have been bruised, scarred and beaten
over time,
But unlike most poems, you can be raw,
You don't have be one of those verses that
can rhyme.
You don't have to be the light to someone,
Or be defined by the clothes that you wore,
Because someone so extravagant yet
complicated,

EVEN GOD HAD TO DIE

Doesn't need to be squeezed inside a
metaphor.
Some people come in your life,
To stay for really long, like a novel,
But when you do find out your worth and
leave,
You realize they were nothing more than a
mere micro tale.
You can be complex and versatile and
beautiful,
You can be worth more than any adjectives
or educational degree,
But you can't ever deny the fact that,
No one can be poetry.

Arkopaul Das

Dont stand over me and cry,
Cos I might be sleeping but I didn't die.
I am in the water that you find in the reef,
I'm the shower that flows through your eyes
When you're suffering in grief.
I'm the stars that twinkle,
The corner of your eyes when you're eighty,
those wrinkles,
I'm in the blood that flows through your
veins,
I'm the sunlight that falls on your glinting
eye,
Or the smell of soil when it rains.
I'm the city's high rush hour and the
weekends low,
I'm what you kiss under, that mistletoe.
I'm that free flock of birds in the air,
I'm in the heart of your lover that she laid
bare.
I'm those miniscule molecules in the air you
breath,
I'm what is real and I'm what is a myth.
I'm that silver lining in the dark clouds of
your mind,

EVEN GOD HAD TO DIE

I'm the belongings you take with yourself,
And I'm the memories you leave behind.
So don't cry over me after all that I said,
I might be gone but I'm not dead.

Arkopaul Das

I wish you could see me now,
I don't know if I've lived up to your
expections,
I don't know if it was a struggle or a lesson.
Clear day of September you brought me my
favorite snack,
Heard you laughing with your friends,
Hole in your heart but still making amends,
Ensured that I got to bed, with a smile,
Told me you were there for me and
I woke up and you were gone.
I wish you could see me now,
Would you even recognise me ?
Would you smile or would you disguise it ?
Would you pat my back when I got to the
top,
Or would have asked me to work harder
Cos I know you would be tough.
You were like death itself and trust me,
I didn't know the concept then but now I do,
A moment you were there and then you
were gone,
Takes forever to build a heart but need just a
moment to have it torn.

You taught me how to be strong,
I literally sat beside you and told everyone,
That Things can't be changed now, that shit
already went wrong,
Only if I knew how much it hurts when you
understand it,
To lose everything before you even had it.
But I just wanna say, it hasn't been easy but
I made it,
I didn't get anywhere but I survived the shit,
With faith in my heart and hope in my soul,
I just wish, you could see me now.

X—X

There's a truth behind the curtains, no one
really knows,
That your heart can stop beating but your
life never slows.
Dare to move the curtain a take a sneak
peak?
You'll see a brutal reality but not the one
that you seek.
It has rivers filled with blood and a
mountain filled with snow,
Its the ones you keep hidden, not the ones
that you show,
It has poison in its root and the leaves has
turned white,
Cos one man's darkness is another man's
light.
There's a truth in this ocean, no one really
knows,
You can drown in it a little or you can go
with the flow.
You'll find the shore ahead and you'll see the
waves rise,
The waves can make you swim faster or
they can be your demise.

There's truth on these walls, no one really
reads,
It has tear stains from the times that didn't
leave you deceased,
It could be a reminder that you have scars in
your past,
Or it could be a sign of the things that made
you, you ;
And why it's worth making your life last.
So do you wanna take a deep dive and see
what else you can find?
Cos this was just a tiny glimpse of the
universe called 'My mind'

X—X

It is so beautiful, all alone,
My heart hasn't seen peace,
Since the day I was born,
It is so beautiful, all alone,
This silence, I call this home.
Countless times I'd lock myself away, lost in
the night,
Pop another pill, saying it's gonna be alright,
I had an aim but for a long time it was outa
my sight,
Didn't give up cos I thought, I might make
it, I just might.
There was a time when I wasn't able to stand

-

Quite literally,
But I don't really talk about it cos who'd
really understand?
I was taught to be grateful, I never tried to
make shit grand,
Live, but never fly so high that you would
forget how to land.
Never met a person who hasn't lied,
Never tried to fit in the "normal" life, which
I was denied,

EVEN GOD HAD TO DIE

I didn't kill myself cos I wanted to say "at
least I tried",
Shed a lotta tears but none when my parents
died.
But shit happens, there is not thing about my
life I would wanna change,
These events, however unfortunate, made
me who I am,
And these, in a way prepared me for the shit
that's yet to come,
Cos, you can tolerate any fucking thing,
when you're numb.
It is so beautiful, sitting in the dark,
There's not a scar on me nor any mark,
It is so beautiful, sitting in the dark ;
All alone, I call this home.

X—X

Back down in the bottomless pit of my
mind,
Where the shadow of you looms beneath,
All these grey, grimy mirages in the sky
forming from diminutive specks of light
trapped
in this eternal darkness of fake solitude
while
the lingering essence of your cologne hangs
and dances in the silence of the midnight,
When the clock struck infinity and kept on
going,
The ashtrays overfilled and bottles of jack
accumulated in the corner,
The chandelier swung like a ballet, keeping
me on her toes,
Swaying and singing in a euphonious
manner,
The hum that hypnotizes my psyche and fills
it with an ardourous vehemence,
Making me forage for you in hunger like a
lunatic,
My demented search for you continues untill
the,

Coruscating luminescence of the star light
floods in through my windows,
And the,
The light flickers overhead, the optical
illusion thinning,
Making me realize you were an illusion after
all,
Yet I weep and crave for a whiff of that
fragrance you intoxicated me with,
Before wandering towards the horizon and
walking off the cliff,
Back down in the bottomless pit of my
mind,
Where the shadow of you looms beneath
these dusty grey mirages in the sky.

X—X

Arkopaul Das

Some nights, I'm trapped inside my mind,
I'm feeling so left behind,
Just don't let me cease away.
When I reach my time, I'll regret leaving
nothing,
To save the day.
Some nights, you would call me up, but it
was all a gimmick,
When I would reach your place, you
wouldn't wanna see me,
The rain would drench me down, I'd wait for
a sign,
Of hope, but the issue, I would never really
get it.
I lagged so far behind after all that you'd
damaged,
I tried be real withchu but you wanted to
change my image,
I never did what you said, why do I still
remember our kisses?
I tried giving you my heart but you returned
it in pieces.
They say go with your gut, don't be trapped
inside your mind,
I'm always tryna be something, I'm always

on my grind,
But falling for people turned me into such a
mess,
I'd rather fall off a bridge right now cos I bet
it'll hurt less.
I still lay down in the park and count all the
stars, like we used to do,
You'd tell me a lot of future plans but none
of them were true,
I passed by the empty crib last night, it still
exists,
Just like me, existing even if I'm down on
my knees.
Some nights I keep staring at the dark
ceiling,
Trying to come to terms with the shit that
I'm feeling,
It would feel like something is dead inside,
and I'd still wanna kill it,
Emotions that break my heart are the ones
that often heal it.
Some nights I'm trapped inside my mind, I
feel so left behind,
Just don't let me cease away,
When I reach my time, help me leave

behind,
Something, to save the day.

X—X

You took me to the edge, and said "This
is the end of the world"
"What do you mean?" I asked,
You pointed at the stars and told me you'd
call,
Maybe I was too dumb to believe that I
wouldn't fall,
My mind was taken away already with the
scent of ethanol. "I believe in you" you said
without a doubt,
You took my hand and laid it out,
The plans of our future, I could hear it nice
and loud,
You smiled and whispered "You did so
much, I'm so proud"
I said that I was nothing, the breeze flew by
us,
The sea gurgled the words unspoken and the
words we should discuss.
Your eyes glittered with the lingering aura
of that love song,
Your hands grazed the back of my neck and
we swayed along,
To the wind, as the lights slowly went out in
the distance,

Arkopaul Das

The city slept but these two hearts were
quite resistant.
You drank the last drop of jack and grinned
in bliss,
Drunk in love', you planted a kiss, on my
lips,
I could taste those fish and the chips,
From earlier when we just had our date,
It was like Chernobyl, radioactive felicity hit
me like those bullets,
But I was unaware of the oncoming eclipse.
Was trying not to be cliche but I ended up
saying that,
You took my sorrow, took my pain, "I think
we should head back" you said, cos it had
started to rain,
I walked you back to your place, and we
kissed again,
It was hard loving you so much and still
staying sane.
I would wait for you for the weeks to come,
You didn't exist for people, dead to some,
No words, no letters, not a sign of your
scent,

I didn't realize when you said end of the world, this is what you meant.

X—X

Arkopaul Das

You can call me when all the lights go out,
But I can't reply now, cos my head is filled
with doubts,
You can't hear me even when I'm crying out,
Screaming till I can't cos that's what life's
been about.
These tears will make me choke and this
darkness will swallow me,
I wish I was blind cos there's so much shit
that I have to see,
With one leg hanging off the edge, I was
grasping on for my life,
I still wasn't sure if I should pull back or
take the fucking dive;
Into the abyss of the dead, carrying all the
debts I didn't pay,
I embraced myself to get pierced with all
things left unsaid,
Fissures in my heart, that's from where I had
bled,
I thought my time has come but I was
terribly misled.
You could call me when it's all said and
done,

EVEN GOD HAD TO DIE

If I'm not hurting for you then it's not really
fun,
You could see that I've always been on the
run,
If I haven't cut you off yet then just wait for
your turn.
With a nod and a smile so many people I
have fooled,
Got away from bs they threw at me and the
shit they tried to pull.
Battered and bruised, I put them in my
muse,
Blood dripping from my arm from all the
times that I got used.
In the end I went down fighting but I
received a fatal blow,
I felt my mind go numb and my heartbeat
started to slow.
I pulled the noose tighter and hung there
from the rope,
I had lost so many people but now I had lost
hope.

x—x

I keep on chasing after, the fragrance of the
dead,
I keep on stumbling over the memories I've
made,
I don't know what I'm after, I don't know
who I am,
So I'm hanging on the best I can,
Hanging on the best I can.
I woke up very next day, drowning in my
own pain,
Last night was starry, my vision blurry,
I think I'm going insane.
Shut the blinds down for a shade, took a few
pills to tame the brain,
All my obsessions, the oberservations,
Beating me at my own game.
And you keep telling me, how to live, how
not drown in sorrow,
Advising me, won't even help, cos I want
this to last some more,
I'll tell you why, I cross each line, knowing
my eventual fate,
And I can't deny, I don't thrive, until I
sedate.

EVEN GOD HAD TO DIE

I keep on chasing after the fragrance of the
dead,
I keep on stumbling over, the memories I've
made,
I don't know what I'm after, I don't know
who I am,
So I'm hanging on the best I can,
Hanging on the best I can.
There's no explanation to how I feel, I don't
try to even conceal,
You say you're sorry, when I'm weary,
I don't know if you're being real.
So many people that I've met, but not a
single one I regret,
Call it resurrection, a reconstruction,
I see none of them as a threat.
And you keep telling me to about the
looming darkness up above,
I know that's true, cos I live there, and that's
the shit I love.
I take a leap of faith, in the clouds, abyss
staring at me,
Silhouetted there, is a paradise, and it's me
who holds the key.
I keep on chasing after, the fragrance of the

dead,
I keep on stumbling over the memories I've
made,
I don't know what I'm after, I don't know
who I am,
So I'm hanging on the best I can,
The best I can.

X——X

The ceiling is so bland on the surface,
But so beautiful when you stare deep within.
So many nooks and crannies, so many
imperfections,
Faded out paint on one side, a crack in the
other corner,
A sense of dampness, with the water seeping
through the roof,
Giving it an abstract bloated shape,
A patch of wetness, sticking out like a sore
thumb.
The fan hung from the ceiling, lifeless and
motionless,
Just like my body would have been,
If it could withstand my weight.
Dirt trapped in the wings of the carbonator,
Colored coppers wires running haywire,
broken, needing repair.
Popping out of of the fibre tubes like veins
in a cancerous body,
The Led bulb on the other end was turned
off,
Because I like to bask in this eternal
darkness.
A spider was crawling towards the nearest

cobweb,
Hanging upside down, trying to trap the
nearest fly.
A dark patch engulfed the space above
window panes,
Where I light an incense stick every
evening.
Creating light just so that it can create
darkness,
An uneven contrast of beliefs and physics
infused together,
The smoke reaching up to the ceiling, trying
to dig through it,
But it can't escape what it's feeling because,
For some people sky might be the limit,
But for us, it's the ceiling.
The ceiling is so bland on the surface,
But so beautiful when you stare deep within,
And embrace it's imperfections piece by
piece,
Just like I'm trying to embrace mine.

x—x

EVEN GOD HAD TO DIE

I think I have to heal this heart again, with
no one by my side,
And it would suck, because you are my one
and only,
My whole world, my pride.
So I got in your car with a heavy heart,
I guess this is it, you had played your part,
I didn't know how to say it, as you started
the car,
I wanted to run away, somewhere where no
one knows me,
Somewhere far.
I could see you not meeting my eyes,
I tried to say something but I didn't know
how to break the ice,
In fact I complimented you and told you,
you look nice,
Cos what are compliments if not hate in
disguise?
I looked ahead at the streets, ignoring my
thoughts,
A mind that fought, a heart that lost,
I wish I could turn back the clock to the
good old times,
Where I wasn't constantly worrying if you

were really mine.
You kept your eyes on the road and barely
gave a chance for me to talk,
I had gone over your insta wondering if I
should have blocked,
I guess it's too late now and I have to
confront these feelings,
Enough of overthinking, enough of staring
at the ceiling.
I decided to go for it, and ask you straight
up,
"I am not feeling the vibe anymore, what's
up?
You give me mixed signals, sometimes you
are there for me,
Sometimes you are not,
What are we? I don't wanna dump this on
you, I know it's a lot"
You just shrugged and said nothing,
Which in turn said a lot of things, held a lot
of meaning,
You slowed down the car and showed me
the door,
Told me you loved me but you didn't feel
the same way no more,

EVEN GOD HAD TO DIE

I turned around and heard you drive away,
I heard you not care, I heard your voice
didn't even break,
And this sucks, because you were my one
and only,
My whole world, my pride,
And yet I have to heal this heart again, with
no one by my side.

X—X

Show me how you feel, show me that it's
real,
Show me that it's worth having hope after
everything.
Show me what I'm worth, show me how to
cope,
Show me how my life ends after everything.
Heart eyes, they were deceiving, I still miss
that feeling,
Tell me from the start, did you even love,
Did you choose to walk away cos you didn't
want my dirt?
Or is it my slurry mind that made the lines
feel blurred.
No, I don't wanna make this hard, but it
don't make sense like art,
Gave my everything and got nothing back,
shit is absurd.
So many emotions to choose from, an a la
Carte,
But it's always the depressing ones that I
preferred.
Passed your crib a couple of times, won't try
to find a word that rhymes,
Didn't even have a dollar or a dime,

Still made sure you'd stay mine.
I saw all of them signs, still chased what still shined,
Now I'm confined, but getting better like an age old wine.
But who knew that, I'd be sidelined,
Things I never did, you turned me into Harvey Weinstein,
Now I gotta get back to work, got to redesign,
Or should I just shoot up the block,
Put my head on a glock and a nine.
Maybe I'll sew it one day, heart to the hemline,
Maybe like a mixed mineral, I'd be able to call her mine,
Something so divine, would be fucking hard to find,
But I won't let my heart get dragged through the mud and put you on a shrine.
Show me how you feel, show me that it's real,
Show me that it's worth having hope after everything.
Show me what I'm worth, show what how to

cope,
Show me how my life ends after everything.

X——X

EVEN GOD HAD TO DIE

And I tell them,
Why love her if you'll let her go,
When you see her, forever doesn't feel like a
myth anymore,
Why love her if you can't take her home,
I might be chasing an impossible dream,
But our love will always stay young.
Sometimes I look back at the things we said,
To each other at 2 am.
Then I'd think of all the efforts that we
made,
Inside it would start to rain.
Sometimes I crumble with this empty heart,
Gave you all and there was nothing left,
Memories of happy ever after,
Keeps searching for you in every form and
shape.
And all the signals you'd give me,
I'd try my best nonetheless,
Sometimes I thought you would leave me,
And that insecurity would fuck with my
head.
All the pills I took, had me trippy,
Just to forget the things you said.

I would have held on, best believe me,
Life became so meaningless.
But all was said and done, we got hurt a ton,
There was nothing to stop us from moving
on,
I would cried out if that would have made
you stay.
And who knew all the right and wrongs,
Would come flowing out in this broken
song,
If only it would have have made you stay.
And all my friends told me to "Walk away,
You deserve way better than what you get,
Block her ass and let her go,
You don't care, she'd soon come to know."
And I tell them,
Why love her if you'll let her go,
When you see forever doesn't feel like a
myth anymore,
Why love her if you can't take her home,
I might be chasing an impossible dream,
But our love will always stay young.

x——x

Scribbling these letters on the wall, I still
ached for that nostalchic essence;
Of a familiar aroma that enchanted me and
taught me a few lessons,
Sozzled out of my mind, with bottles of jack
accumulated in the corner,
Reeking of an appaling miasma, I have lost
my honour,
These four walls has been my alter of
solitude and sorrow,
Despondency hung from the ceiling, poison
dripped from this pen,
Stupefied with the lack of reverence for my
own self, hoping it will disappear by
tomorrow.
But I'm falling in this dark abyss of nihility,
the wind whipping past me,
In the state of free fall, is where I've felt the
most carefree, but,
It's amalgamated with an ardourous
inclination to bless; you
With a dagger lacerating through your
toxicity, call it my very own coup de gràce.
I'll be your quietus and this bailey is your
death missive and;

Arkopaul Das

I'll be at my castle of fortitude, a spear up
your spine is what you shall receive,
Swiftly I perceived the dangling stars on the
ceiling,
My enthusiasm to eradicate you is because
of this hurt that I've been conceiling,
I can't anymore, you're always at the door,
I've yelled at you so many times my throat
has gotten sore,
Reminscing your memories has severed my
heart from the carcass,
Black eyes, vertiginous state of mind has
turned my life into a circus,
Yearning for the presence that I abhor but I
love,
How I wish for those burnished fingers to
graze against my scruff,
But I'm stuck in the prison of my mind,
drowning in this dolorous ocean of
desolation,
Claustrophobia gripping my nerves, my eyes
went through dilation,
The walls were closing in so I embraced this
penitentiary of loneliness,
If I didn't pick up the pen, my mind would

implode and I'd be gone without a trace.
Still haunted by your memories, I stared at
the wall going through convalescence,
Scribbling these letters on the wall, I still
ached for that nostalgic essence.

Arkopaul Das

We are headed in the black hole of life,
the void,
Will you hold my hand,
Help me walk over these treacherous
trenches
Of sheer agony and misery.
Where the living souls die and turn into
mist,
Into pure nothingness, their energies
dispersed,
That's why the air is so heavy, that's why it's
so hard to breath.
There's fire and smoke everywhere,
Yet we are in an endless vaccum,
A cosmos transcending space and time,
Life and death,
Just you, me and this black hole called life,
Slowly swallowing us all. Slowly
succumbing to humanity,
To civilization. Demons breathing down our
necks,
Pushing us onwards, there is no respite,
No choice, no options, just you and me,
Bound together, so close yet oceans apart,
We can barely even see each other. Touch

each other,
Because your love is poison, and so am I.
Perfectly contrasted, perfectly balanced,
Like sand to sea, coexisting, and moving in
this black hole of life,
With stars and supernovas, nebulas and
galaxies,
Light years and years apart, yet so close,
Aligning together, fitting in like a puzzle
piece,
That needs to be solved.
That needs to be treated, to be felt, to be
loved,
Alone and lonely, with nothing but
blackness, and distant
Streaks of light, for company.
With nothing but the inner demons, urging
us on,
Pushing us in the black hole of life, the void.

X—X

I heard what's going on, you are the talk of
town,
Wanna go out? Cos if you agree I'm down,
I heard what's going on, you're the talk of
town,
Pretty girls like you should never have to
frown.

I heard you're hard to get, but I can't forget,
Everytime I laid my eyes on you I went
crazy,
Was it last night's text, or was it the day we
met?
Damn, can't even think straight my mind so
hazy.
And all those sweet nothings that you'd
whisper in my ear,
All those times I hugged you when you were
holding back tears,
And the days we spent driving around all
night,
The way I'd be sad the moment you were
our of sight.

I heard you are the talk of town, so tells
what's going?
I wanna take you out so lemme know if
you're down,
I heard what's going on, you are the talk of
town,
I'd buy you a bunch of flowers with a gown.

I don't know how it happened, it just
happened so fast,
Every moment I spend with you, I wanna
make it last,
All the things you do, I don't even know
how,
I thought I'd never catch feelings but I
I'm deep in it now.
Girl, I know your dms blowing up from
people better than me,
When you post your pics with your friends I
wish it could be me,
I wanna listen to you talk for hours about
your life,
While I day dream how beautiful you'd look
as my wife.
I know I'm not best, I got issues like the rest,

Maybe too much that I'd wanna get off of
my chest,
I know it won't be easy but I'm ready to
fight,
Cos one thing I know for sure is how to treat
a girl right.

I heard what's going on, you're the talk of
town,
Wanna go out? cos if you agree I'm down,
I heard what's going on, you're the talk on of
town,
Pretty girls like should never have to frown.

X—X

Give her some freedom for she will fly,
If you go back in history women have left
poignant marks that you can't deny,
First off, division of labour needs to be
under scrutiny,
Fuck your age old mindset that biology is
destiny.
She's more than just a pretty face or an
anatomy you can use,
How often do you hear about males getting
oppressed in the news?
Gone are the male dominant days of the
world, she's a self tagged vixen,
She deserves to rule the world not stay in the
kitchen.
In a lot of places, women are prohibited
from acquiring property rights
And the capitals they should be getting,
Women of colour are often looked down
upon in job settings,
Cases get overruled and goes against true
testaments,
And apparently only men are beneficial for
sustainable development.
1.7 million new born deaths occur due to

lack of health services or ration,
At least 200 million women every year
becomes a part of female genitalia
mutilation.
Ignorant males these days scorns at
empowerment issues just to thrive,
There are countries in the world where
women are not allowed to drive.
While your sneer at the word feminism to
look edgy and cool,
Just to protect themselves form violence,
hundreds of women had to protest in
Istanbul.
Fuck that, how often to do you get
deprecated due to your gender, weight or
shape?
How often do you hear males being a victim
of marital rape?
Even their autonomy over their own body
gets questioned, cos of the promiscuity they
projects,
How often do you hear males get called a
slut just cos he had sex.
You think you're being discriminated against
cos society asks men to not show feelings,

While thousands of female fetuses are
buried in garbage due to acts of vengeance,
And honor killings.
Even then, women has left a mark in the
fields of physics, humanities, chemistry and
science,
Feminism has shifted the position of women
in a society and made them self reliant,
The skirmish for justice is over, the war of
equality has been fought,
Remember there's not a thing a man can do
that a woman cannot.

X—X

Take me back, way back, way way back to
the first time,
When I found myself laying in bed
wondering where I went wrong this time.
When I took a bunch of pills, and passed out
alone this time,
Come Monday, I was back on the bus going
to school like I'm not dead inside.
Didn't know it before but I could hide, my
real emotions from the prying eyes,
From your friends who are snakes in
disguise,
Come the night, you'll drink to your demise.
Sometimes you have to distance yourself
from the sinners,
Never lost at life, but still didn't come out a
winner.
With a heavy throat you call out in a,
screech that sounds like it's ringing,
You call in sick cos of the show you're
binging.
Take me back, way back, way way back, to
the first time,
When I was crossing a lane and wished I
would get hit by a car,

When i didn't discover lil peep, still
jamming to cole and lemar,
Come to think of it, they still the only ones
who got real bars.
But that's a side note, getting distracted as
usual, I know,
People get highs and lows in their life but I
got lows and low,
Falling apart and your eyes can't even see
me,
I'm an angel, tryna get to heaven, and you
can't be me.
Sometimes it gets sunny but mostly it rains,
Tears come from my heart, not from my
brain.
And you if lived my life, you'd be driven
insane,
No one really cares not even when
something shitty happens.

x—x

And I tell them,
Why love her if you'll let her go,
When you see her, forever doesn't feel like a
myth anymore,
Why love her if you can't take her home,
I might be chasing an impossible dream,
But our love will always stay young.
Sometimes I look back at the things we said,
To each other at 2 am.
Then I'd think of all the efforts that we
made,
Inside it would start to rain.
Sometimes I crumble with this empty heart,
Gave you all and there was nothing left,
Memories of happy ever after,
Keeps searching for you in every form and
shape.
And all the signals you'd give me,
I'd try my best nonetheless,
Sometimes I thought you would leave me,
And that insecurity would fuck with my
head.
All the pills I took, had me trippy,
Just to forget the things you said.
I would have held on, best believe me,

EVEN GOD HAD TO DIE

Life became so meaningless.
But all was said and done, we got hurt a ton,
There was nothing to stop us from moving
on,
I would cried out if that would have made
you stay.
And who knew all the right and wrongs,
Would come flowing out in this broken
song,
If only it would have have made you stay.
And all my friends told me to "Walk away,
You deserve way better than what you get,
Block her ass and let her go,
You don't care, she'd soon come to know."
And I tell them,
Why love her if you'll let her go,
When you see forever doesn't feel like a
myth anymore,
Why love her if you can't take her home,
I might be chasing an impossible dream,
But our love will always stay young.

X—X

I don't really stress about what I write,
I don't stress about my image, I don't stress
if I die,
I try to be open, I got nothing to hide,
It's not easy when you wanna stab the back
of your head and take it out through your
eye,
I've fucked over and been fucked over, I
won't lie.
Yeah sometimes I'm humble and sometimes
i can be cocky,
I mix facts with fiction cos I wanna be real
but keep shit lowkey.
I write shit down and then burn em cos I
ain't tryna make it big,
I can call people out but I ain't tryna take a
dig,
Rolled a lotta joints but never lit a cig,
And if you feel what I'm sayin, lemme know
you fuck with my shit.
Yeah I been insecure and immature,
But you also an axe body spray acting like
Christian Dior,
Well you know how it is, life treated me like
a whore,

I'm at that point in my life where either you
get me or there's the door.
There been people everywhere telling me to
redeem myself,
There been times when I would be alone
tryna kill myself,
I had written down shit that had happened
since my birth, in form of a list,
But who do I redeem myself to since God
doesn't exist?

X—X

Arkopaul Das

Hey there kids want to follow this balloon?
If you follow it right you'll find a drain soon.
When you peek down the grills you'll see a
clown,
You'll see the face smiling, you'll never find
me frown.
I'll tell you all the fantasies and make you
believe in fairy tales,
I'll give you this candy and tiny little
jingling bells,
When stretch out your hand to grab it from
me,
I'll bite it off and hunt you when you sleep.
I'll show you your darkest fears and make
you scream,
You'll see my eyes when you are awake and
even when you dream.
I'll lead you to my lair, putting you in a
trance,
You'll have the front row seats of the stage
where I dance.
I'll enter your blood stream and feed on you,
from the inside,
I'm like a parasite stuck in your mind, there's
nowhere you can hide.

And just when you think you've gotten rid of
me,
I'll scrape the skin of your face and chop
your head off like a tree.
I'll rip your intestines out and light the end
of it like a dynamite.
Your guts will explode over your
insecurities, and then it'll be night.
Now you're just a carcass of a sinner so
filled with greed,
I'll dangle you from the ceiling just to watch
you slowly bleed.
So, boy, you can't escape until you're driven
insane,
Only way to get rid of me is to put a bullet
through your brain.

X—X

Arkopaul Das

Stop being insecure, you're beautiful,
Cos beauty lies in actions.
It's about being able to care in a world
that needs you to be selfish,
That needs to you compete with each other,
And belittle each other,
In order to get to the top.
I refuse to compete.
Beauty lies in caring,
In being faithful and loyal,
And looking out for people and yourself.
Beauty lies in that one time you gave food to
a street dog,
Or helped someone go through tough times,
Or when you didn't cuss someone out, who
did you wrong,
Or even when you held a door for someone,
Cos,
Beauty is in the smallest of things,
Moments, that you create ,
With yourself, with people you love,
And with complete strangers sometimes,
Doing what you wanna do,
Being spontaneous and calm,

Flying and drowning at the same time,
In the love that you have for yourself,
And for others,
In this cruel world,
Now that's what you call beauty.

X—X

Sometimes you feel the highs in life and then the lows. Just like heart beat, goes up and down, and when it stops , you die. For me it went down, and down, while I'm pretending like it's going up. I feel like… I don't really know what I'm writing right now, I'm way too drowsy and fucked, probably gonna make grammatical errors for the first time in my life.

And you know what, as much shit I've been through, I wouldn't trade my life for the world. I wouldn't change it given the chance, I wouldn't want a better life. I've learnt so many valuable things in this life when I was shoved into a pile of trauma from the get go. It's so easy for everyone to judge and criticise and assume and hate, not that it's anything new for me, I'm used to it. I'm numb to it. I just wish there was some way I could put them in my place.

If some fucking genie appeared in my hallucinations and asked me what I wanna wish for then this is exactly what I wanna wish for.

Put them in my shoes and make em walk half a mile. Let them see the responsibility's I have while icarry a load of shit on my back.

They will scream and cry and run the fuck away from this lie and probably fucking kill themselves. Trust me, they will.

It's scary in my head, it's hopeless in my life. But I don't like complaining, I will pick myself up no matter what, put bandage on my bruises and move the fuck ahead. Anyway, it's like 3 am right now.

And I'm still not home yet. Sitting outside the emergency room, there's an apartment building in front of me, with a light glowing inside a room. Someone is awake even at this hour, is that a gamer, an engineer or is that a reflection of me?

X—X

You are an oasis in the middle of my
desert,
You're the only thing alive in this graveyard,
How I wish I could tell how much I love
you,
But the voices in my head tells me don't tell
her.
My mentality is actually getting sick,
Longing for that true connection makes me
feel weak,
I wish I could describe the rollercoaster of
the emotions I been feeling,
Burying it down my throat I can barely even
speak.
Still remember our journey so far,
Sit in front of the river or laugh out in my
car,
Happiness struck me like a lightning in the
darkness,
Little did you know inside me I was waging
a cold war.
I don't got so many friends, they are mostly
far and few,
My heart was a tree leaf and you sat on it
like the morning dew,

I mostly live alone, trying to cling on to
some hope,
You saw a thousand problems in me but I
couldn't spot a single flaw in you.
I feel like I've won the battle, but at what
cost?
Every piece of me feels broken, bruised and
lost,
I can see the morning sun rising over the
blood spattered battlefield,
People you love would be the ones to hurt
you the most.
I'm back in this desert and I'm dying,
Thirsting for a drop of hope, I don't know
how I'm surviving,
My vision is getting blurry, and I see
mirages in the distance,
The Oasis has disappeared and my thoughts
are unforgiving.

X—X

I keep the phone away for a minute, and
stare into the darkness,
Heart broken apart, couldn't see a future to
be honest,
The serotonin hit from the same three apps
aren't working anymore,
I keep fighting to stay alive while death
keeps knocking at my door.
I look around, my dark room's a mess just
like my head,
I see the blue light of my laptop, only source
of light I had left,
I see the Benzo's and xanax pills strewn on
the table,
A bottle of jack lying in the corner, I had
taken off the label.
I get up from my bed and grab a few of them
pills,
Is today the day I finally give up, the day I
finally kill?
I can't breath, my knees weak, eyes blurry,
I try to speak to myself but can't, my voice is
slurry,
I grab half a dozen Benzo's and the water

bottle,
I take a deep breath, this is it, it is settled,
The walls feel like they are closing in on me,
bile rising to my throat,
The people you love would be the one to
hurt you the most.
I toss the bottle away and swallow the pills
dry,
I saunter to that one corner of the bed where
I usually lie,
Looking up at the ceiling, the ceiling staring
back at me,
Slowly losing vision, the demons would
finally let me be,
I would finally be set free, free of all the
pain and hurt,
Losing control over myself, my mind
struggling to stay alert.
Maybe I passed out, I don't know, but I
woke up sick and nauseas,
Ran to the washroom, grabbed the sink and
threw up,
Sick to my stomach.
I washed my face and came back inside,
realising I've failed,

Arkopaul Das

I could see the sun rising up, it's a new day
with same old shit,
And here we go again.

X—X

EVEN GOD HAD TO DIE

She is an illusion, a magic, a part of thou,
Glides down my body, sometimes she sits
on my skin,
Like a drop of dew on a sunflower,
That turns its head around to find that hint of
gaiety,
After a rainy winter morning,
When the sun finally glistens and rids
herself,
Of the gloomy clouds, and shines down on
you,
When the first ray of hope lingers on your
petals,
As the drop glissades down and falls
headfirsts,
In an abyss, filled with treasures, that;
Binds you in a trance of solitude,
Loaded with glimmer of hopes and dreams,
Of a better life,
Every pore of your skin enrages, with fire
and,
A frigid insecurity of losing a beauty,
Such as her.
But my heart always desires what it can't
possess,

Arkopaul Das

Of what is beyond my realm,
For she flies high, like an unicorn shredding
through a rainbow,
Reaching a state of nirvana of blessedness,
Leaving little droplets of coruscating shells,
Ones the high tide can't wash away, ones the
salty water can't weather,
Dazzling in an ocean filled with stars,
Only to be acquired by a shabby person like
thine truly.
I still look at the sky to catch a glimpse of
that shooting star,
Of that longing essence of fairy dust,
While I caress the shell, that
metamorphosized my being,
And commended me with an aura of pure
euphoria,
Changing my life,
I have become that ray of gaiety,
And the sunflowers turn to me now,
For she's an illusion, a magic, a part of thou.

X—X

EVEN GOD HAD TO DIE

Back in the day, when we were young,
We would play a game called hide and seek.
I was never the one to close my eyes
And count to ten.
I was always the one to run away and
squeeze myself,
In the smallest space available,
And crouch there uncomfortably, waiting to
be found.
I realized even now, we are all doing it,
Every moment, every second of the day.
We are all running away from our fears,
From attachments, from our loved ones,
From our ambitions, passions,
Closing off our eyes and ears, and ignoring
the people
Calling our names.
I could never be the one to find people,
I never felt like it would be worth it.
I never tried to look for the people hiding,
Cos I felt like they are sitting there
comfortably,
While I'm the one putting all the effort.
But now that I'm on the other side of the
tide,

Waiting and waiting, to be found,
To be held and to be understood,
To be loved and cared for,
To finally break down all the barriers and
give in,
I realized I want to be the one who puts
himself out there,
Find the ones who needs nurturing,
Fill their veins with my own ecstasy,
And make the world a better place.

X—X

As I sit in my dark room,
I hear the rain and thunder
Howling outside,
I hear them whisper in my ear,
The words that you are thinking,
I hear the burden everyone's carrying,
Through the wind lashing on my windows,
I hear the city grow quieter,
But even through this hypnotic noise,
Of the raindrops on the glass, I can still hear
the souls that cry.
They say the wind carries all the hurt,
That people have faced,
And takes them away,
Otherwise how can something invisible,
Can be powerful enough to make my
window sway?
I wish you were by my side,
Telling me stories that only the wind knew,
Why is the air, the thunder, the rain,
Why is everything,
Reminding me of you?

X—X

EVEN GOD HAD TO DIE

I don't want your fake hellos or those fake
smiles,
I don't want those small talk that stretches
on for miles.
I don't want to hear about your perfect life,
Or how you could make a perfect wife.
I don't want to see your contoured face,
Or hear about your expensive condo in some
exotic place.
I don't wanna hear you talk about your cool
friends,
Or ramble on about the latest fashion trends,
I've always been someone who would look
deeper behind the veil,
Hear those voices in you and the secrets they
tell.
I wanna see the you after you wake up,
After you break up,
I wanna see the you who's tired of keeping
on the facade,
Hold you,
When you cry on the floor at 2 in the
morning every week,
With Jack Daniel's in one hand and a

mascara smeared cheek,
I wanna know about your past, all your
darkest memories,
I wanna be the one to tell our kids all these
fucked up stories.
I wanna hear you vent and rant, and let out
all your imperfections,
Talk about your wildest desires and all your
passions.
I wanna stick with the real you forever,
And be the one to tell you that sometimes
you are beautiful,
And sometimes you are a mess,
But one thing that will never change is,
You'd forever be my beautiful mess
regardless.

X—X

ARKOPAUL DAS

We live thinking this is an unconfined
world,
Like we are independent,
Like we could vanquish the atrocities,
Spread our wings and fly high,
Until someone tells us that it's not right.
We are taught to believe,
We are taught to follow a set of given rules,
Even when they don't make sense,
We are asked to have faith, supplicate and
pray,
To a greater power.
We are asked not to sin,
Yet sadistic rituals in the name of sacrifices,
Are made everyday.
Marriage, confirmation or ordination,
Rites demonstrate reverence they say,
Yet they often lead to barbarity,
When science breaks them down with logic
and facts,
Pointing out the absurdity it enacts,
Postulate conjectures with well cerebral
facts and instil certainty,
Or write a book based on your empirical
credence,

And get half of the world on your side?
Then they sit down to discuss why our youth
today,
Aren't as exultant, but yet they are so
liberated,
But the bottom line is,
Follow the path and let your individualistic
happiness be obliterated.
Welcome to world of religion.

X—X

ARKOPAUL DAS

After barely surviving the constant
torture,
He clutched the bottle tightly in his hand,
He thought about his idol and his departure,
The man had worked his ass off,
Day and night without a break, yet they'd
scoff,
The machine would churn,
His subconscious would burn,
Every time he got it wrong, he would know
time is running out,
But it was only him who could make the
bombe,
It was only him who could break the code.
And so he did after years of struggle,
Alan Turing Helped them win,
Just to end up costing his life to the
discriminatory laws,
Which they considered a sin.
Gulping the bitter liquid,
His realization was still vivid -
That, even after so many years of growth
and development,
Conservative minds still persists in various
parts of the world,

There was no way he could make a dent.
He just happened to get caught up in
between.
Before he passed out,
There was only one thought his mind was on
about,
If a country could kill a guy who won them
the war,
Who was he to live?

X—X

His course hands caressed her skin ever
so romantically,
Only to grope her breasts, eyes full of
melancholy,
His other hand slithered down her face to
her throat,
Clasped her thorax hard as if crumpling a
worthless note,
She gasped for breath, unable to break free,
He murmured "shh this is love you see?"
Thrashed against the wall, her hands were
bound,
Her eyes wailed agony but her mouth
couldn't make a sound,
She gave out a loud scream as she was
penetrated,
When she said the vows she never thought
her dignity would be donated,
Like a tangled mess she lay there,
Contemplating life, her body which is his,
laid bare,
Nights went by fast, she couldn't take it
anymore,
She decided to take a stand,
But wherever she went she was shown the

door,
Turns out impartiality is a fantasy while
justice is a folklore,
She knew the vertical noose was the only
way out of here,
When the world kicked her rear,
And whispered in her ear,
It's not rape when you're married, dear.

X—X

ARKOPAUL DAS

Last time I checked you hated me,
I know why,
I made you crave for his love harder,
Broke you down just to make you stronger.
I'm always in between,
A looming presence, there but unseen,
I make you insecure, giving you sleepless
nights,
I make you cry and weep,
When you miss him under the moonlight,
In joy or in pain,
Sometimes you'd feel fed up and go insane.
But I'm just giving you a chance,
To think it over,
No chances for unwanted hook ups,
When you aren't really sober,
Cos I'll be there, to support you,
To make your heart long for the one who's
true,
Until eventually I bid adieu.
While you bury those negative ideologies
about romance,
Then you see him, here's your chance,
Overjoyed,

You advance, kiss his lips, and dance,
Did I even even introduce myself?
They call me distance.

X—X

One time she stole something from her
mate,
She was beat up,
God is watching, they said,
She learned to pray at an early age,
Her dreams were to bring peace,
To the poor souls hidden in this broken
maze,
Days went by,
People preached at her, she didn't
understand why,
One day, she held his hand,
That's when the first star would land,
His finger was still stuck between her little
palm,
The rest of him was blown away into pieces
and then some,
She heard an uproar, an hidden rage,
Smoke and dust made her feel dazed,
Until the impending volcano rose high up,
In the sky,
And she knelt down and prayed,
Not for her, but for the wounded and the
dead,
Cries everywhere, fireballs would rain,

Syria was never the same again,
She wanted to help them, but how?
She wondered, is God watching now?

X—X

Don't you hate me,
For the shit that I did,
Give me a chance to,
Be in your memories,
Don't you make me,
Empathize or guilty,
Try to envision the,
Life that I have lived.
I know I've,
Been immature and caused a lot of hurt,
I know I've,
Failed you when we could have made fresh
start,
I know I wasn't the best.
But when you feel so forlorn,
Forget those hearts that I've torn,
Keep my soul close to yours,
And I'll never be gone.
And when you become desolate,
Trying to fill the gap that I've left,
Hear my voice,
Sing those words, that I always wanted to
say.
Now don't hate me,

For the shit that makes you, miss,
For we will meet in,
Another life, better than this.

X—X

Since the birth of earth people has been worrying about their looks.

Some people argues that no matter how much of a personality you have, for great first impressions or for someone to fall in love with you at first sight, looks are like compulsory.
But think about it, do you actually need to make a good first impression to people you meet?

It's not a job interview. It's not a school, or an exam hall or some place with authority. It's probably just some guy or girl you want to be friends with, whom you don't even know; so ask yourself why do you have to care if you had made a good impression anyway?
Let me tell you something.

The people who fall in love at first side are the ones who breaks up after a month. If it's so easy to fall in then it's as easy to fall out of it for them.

You don't want these people to begin with. Yes you are probably messed or "unattractive", but trust me, you are better of people like this let alone try to impress them.

You need people who'd actually know you are a mess and be ready to bear with you and handle you anyway.

These people are rare and it takes time, if you haven't met them yet, you will. Hang tight and live your life, free of worries.

X—X

They say you'll never find closure,
While holding back to the old ones
You will rise high up in the air,
Just to fall down again.
Now grades define your intelligence,
While looks define your popularity,
As I try to trudge my way through this
utmost diligence,
I see souls living trivial lives without clarity.
It's high up there,
And we are killing ourselves to get there at
the top,
All the colors remixing to make a negligent
bind,
It would still look like it didn't have any
purpose even it I were blind,
There's no way to stop now, we are too far
in,
Care is a myth while kindness is a sin,
Chase and compete and die and repeat,
That's what this life means.
But what's the purpose of it all?
No one has a second to stop and imagine.
I don't wanna find any closer,

I don't wanna move on from the old ones
No I don't wanna rise up or fall now,
Ill be fine as I was, again.

X—X

ARKOPAUL DAS

You're 30,
You wake up, and think, why,
Get ready and go to work place,
Make fake faces and lie,
Dark eyes, feeling hollow, stressed,
Living the formulaic life,
Is this what you wanna do?
You have friends, you laugh,
Cracking jokes in the cafeteria isn't tough,
Then hit the club after work hours,
Groove to the beats, have champagne
showers,
Live the formulaic life.
Is this what you wanna do?
You come home, drained out,
Both physically and emotionally,
You don't even have a dog to greet you,
Because you have never been good at
caring,
You undress and fall back on your bed,
exhausted,
Having everything,
Living like everybody else, yet
Feeling so empty inside,
Asking yourself constantly,

EVEN GOD HAD TO DIE

Is this what I wanna do?
But right now you're not 30, yet,
You still get sad, you get happy, you have
dreams, you fall in love,
So,
Don't give up on your dreams and hopes,
Don't give up on your family, your studies,
Your passions or your girlfriend,
Cos if you do, one day, you will ask
yourself,
Is this what I really wanna do?

X—X

I stood there watching the waves come and
go,
The paper sticking to my palm like thrones,
My pain blossomed into poetry and
I bled words on them,
When I finally decided to let go.
They say the sea brings everything back,
As I tossed my aching heart in the water,
Hoping it will reach you on the other side
Of the horizon,
Hoping you are standing there looking at the
star lit
Water on the other side,
Waiting for my soul to reach you.
As you read the blurred clumsy words,
I would bleed out here and disappear in the
ocean,
Of your love.
Because you are like the sky and I'm like the
ocean,
We never meet until the sun sets on the
horizon.
Oddly both the sky and the water become
crimson,

Like my blood flowing through this earth,
Flowing through you,
Because even if I'm gone my words will
stay,
Etched in every pore of this world and,
Etched in your heart forever.

X—X

Joy is such a tricky subjective word.
What's joy really?
Is it the smile that's pasted on your lips
When you talk to your people?
Is it a midnight call with the person you
love?
Is it getting good grades, or earning money?
Is it about success, is it about being famous?
Is it seeing your family happy?
Have you ever sat down and wondered,
What really is joy?
Is it more of a personal feeling,
Is it soothing a heart that isn't healing?
Is it fighting wars or saving humanity,
How would you do that when you're filled
with insanity?
Is it dancing in the rain,
Or getting married to your crush
Or when your child finally clasps your
finger and smiles.
Or that kick of LSD, that ecstasy rush?
We all think we have found our joy,
But have we?

Cos joy is such a tricky subjective word,
What's joy really?

X—X

Everyone who is not afraid of rejection,
Of failures, but of affection,
Of pain and heartache,
Of remaining awake,
Has been rejected countless times
and has been beaten down,
Has had sleepless nights,
With no one by their side.
Everyone who is a loner,
Who walks alone, and avoids the crowd,
Was once the most approachable person,
Until circumstances pushed him,
Back to his own little shell,
As a method of preserving oneself from shit.
Everyone who is afraid to love,
Afraid to lay out their heart and trust,
In people, in himself,
Was once the one to make flowers blossom,
With love and honesty,
Until his heart broke,
And the world slapped his face,
With betrayal and dishonesty.
Everyone who is not afraid to die,
Has been through extreme trauma,

EVEN GOD HAD TO DIE

Maybe mental, emotional, physical,
Has seen deaths and destruction of himself,
And of loved ones,
But don't think that,
He isn't afraid to die cos he's strong,
Cos he's a warrior, no,
He isn't afraid, because he's already dead.

X—X

Does it bother you, that nothing matters?
Does it bother,
That you never get to see the real you?
Because every time you look at yourself
In the mirror,
The image is always reversed.
Does it bother
That someone else has your name?
Someone who is probably quite opposite
than you,
Someone who might even be commiting
unthinkable things,
Yet he or she bears your name?
Does it bother,
That there's a different perception of you,
In everyone's mind?
No one really knows you,
Hell even you don't know who you are.
All of them think you are something you
aren't,
And so do you,
But who are you?
Does it bother,
That you are floating on a giant rock,
In a big dark vacuum?

Does it bother,
That the thing you are worrying about the
most,
Doesn't matter to the rest the city, country,
Or the universe?
What you're worrying about,
Won't even matter to you, in five years?
My point is, we all live trivial lives,
When you compare it in the broader
spectrum,
No matter how world ending it might feel
like right now,
Just take a deep breath, and let it go.
Cos it simply doesn't matter.

X—X

It's not easy to be in touch with your
emotions ,
When you are up and running with your life,
Constabtly keeping a straight face on, and
hide,
From the judgemental glares,
Devoiding yourself of any feelings.
It's never good to remain one dimensional
like a robot,
Like the world expects us to be ,
Always happy and doing what they want,
Because for real shit builds up inside even
when we don't notice,
No matter how positive you try to be,
The world will always punch your face ,
And give you reasons to give up until you
actually die,
So don't pretend it's all good.
Don't pretend like you have never made
mistakes,
Like you are the victim, cos it happens to
almost everyone.
Sit back and cry if needed,
Take your time to get over certain things

instead of
Denying what you really feel.
Remember sadness is an art,
When sadness flows through your veins you
get to ;
Channel it into something productive,
And bring out that creative side of you,
Which you didn't even know, existed.
Be sad or weak or even vulnerable,When
necessary,
it's normal human reactions
To a fucked up situation and it's really okay,
But once you get over it, get your swag back
on,
And hussle till you are at the top.

X—X

ARKOPAUL DAS

I think I have to heal this heart again, with
no one by my side,
And it would suck, because you are my one
and only,
My whole world, my pride.
So I got in your car with a heavy heart,
I guess this is it, you had played your part,
I didn't know how to say it, as you started
the car,
I wanted to run away, somewhere where no
one knows me,
Somewhere far.
I could see you not meeting my eyes,
I tried to say something but I didn't know
how to break the ice,
In fact I complimented you and told you,
you look nice,
Cos what are compliments if not hate in
disguise?
I looked ahead at the streets, ignoring my
thoughts,
A mind that fought, a heart that lost,
I wish I could turn back the clock to the
good old times,
Where I wasn't constantly worrying if you

were really mine.
You kept your eyes on the road and barely
gave a chance for me to talk,
I had gone over your insta wondering if I
should have blocked,
I guess it's too late now and I have to
confront these feelings,
Enough of overthinking, enough of staring
at the ceiling.
I decided to go for it, and ask you straight
up,
"I am not feeling the vibe anymore, what's
up?
You give me mixed signals, sometimes you
are there for me,
Sometimes you are not,
What are we? I don't wanna dump this on
you, I know it's a lot"
You just shrugged and said nothing,
Which in turn said a lot of things, held a lot
of meaning,
You slowed down the car and showed me
the door,
Told me you loved me but you didn't feel
the same way no more,

I turned around and heard you drive away,
I heard you not care, I heard your voice
didn't even break,
And this sucks, because you were my one
and only,
My whole world, my pride,
And yet I have to heal this heart again, with
no one by my side.

X—X

EVEN GOD HAD TO DIE

I'm done,
Done with all this loneliness,
I'm done, done with all the mess I've made.
Broke so many friendships, now I'm alone,
Met so many people but they are all gone,
Sitting here, wondering how fucked I am,
Where do I go from here?
I have no one to back on, people are a scam.
I look around and I see them all so happy,
I stand there wondering, why couldn't I be
them?
Why do I lose everytime, as if my life is a
game.
I cower back to the darkness that embraces
me,
I hide my feelings from the people who
faces me,
I am tired of pretending like everything is
fine,
I wish I could go buy a glock and a nine.
I'm done,
Done with all this loneliness,
I'm done, done with all the hate I get.
They ask me why I am acting weird,
You'd know if if you actually cared,

ARKOPAUL DAS

They tell me how everything's gonna be
fine,
How do I explain I'm constantly exploding
like a landmine.
I haven't felt happiness for a day in my life,
I haven't had day when I didn't wanna stab
myself with a knife,
I'm fighting every moment trying to hold on,
But to what end?
Life keeps going on.
It doesn't get better, everyday it gets worse,
Every day gets harder I can barely stay
afloat,
I'm trying to stay on the surface gasping for
air,
But no one held out their hand cos no one's
there.
I'm done.
Done with all the loneliness,
I'm done, done with all the mess I've made.

X—X

You feel like you're dropping down a
deep dark abyss,
There's no hope for you out there, no people
you'd miss,
You slowly lose interests in everything you
loved,
Your cries go unheard, your dreams are
shattered, you end up feeling misjusdged.
Your mind is possessed with an
uncontrollable fit of frustration,
Barely concious anymore, you decide to
teach the society a lesson.
People losing lives, but our society has still
not accepted,
It rages on worldwide, with around 264
million people affected.
We hail feminism, romanticize politics, and
fight over our borders,
While 85% of people in low income
countries receive no treatment for this
disorder.
Centered on the legalities, the healthcare
system is corrupt,
Even after so long it's seen as a tainted
social construct.

We are always backed up in the corner with
studies, work and responsibilities,
Or the careers we would pursue,
36% of Indians will fall prey to major
depression at some point in their lives, says
WHO,
No, none of them they are cowards, they
probably fought till the end bravely,
In 2012, an average of 371 Indians
commited suicide, daily.
We are taken advantage off, forced into
formalities, sometimes without our consent,
According to WHO, the major contributors
of depression are - biological, social, and
psychological trauma, unemployment and
breavement.
Tangled in our own hate, discrimation and
our hunt for moral supremacy,
We negate the prevalent issues, and
disregard suicidal traits,
33% of Indians commit suicide by poison,
26% by hanging, and 9% of them self-
immolates.
Enervated voices are shut, thoughts are
sealed and mouths are taped,

EVEN GOD HAD TO DIE

Depression and suicidal tendencies are
stigmatized to the point where it could be
compared to marital rape.
If you feel you're at edge, at the tail end of
your journey,
Remember you'll leave behind someone or
the other, who'll be mourning.
You might feel you're alone, but there's
always someone for everyone,
Save your loved ones and yourself, call
09152987821.

X—X

I pick up the pen again, losing all my
patience,
Losing my grip on life, and all my grace and
cadence.
Morning brings me hope, but every night is
a fucking torture,
I'm tired of fighting, for once I want to be
fought for.
End it with poison, or maybe with a knife,
I'm sad but I smile, and that has been my
life.
It's hard to pretend all the time, I might
actually go mad,
But smiling is far easier than explaining why
I'm sad.
Every moment I live is a battle, every breath
I take is a war,
And it's unfortunate, or maybe fortunate,
that I'm not winning anymore.
A million efforts still won't bring me the
happiness, I know cos I've tried,
A million tears won't bring me closure, I
know cos I've cried.
I scrap up the broken pieces, tryna conjure

up something,
I've felt so much, now I wanna feel nothing.
People keep telling me that life will go on
you gotta give it a headstart,
But I'm tired, and I want it to end, that's the
saddest part.
I learnt to accept the truth, this is what I get,
I can't make demands,
Sometimes you've to be okay with falling
apart while nobody understands.
I don't wanna always be happy, that will
lead to chaos and madness,
Will the word happiness even make sense if
its not contrasted with sadness?
I am not afraid to lose myself giving more
than I receive,
Greatest loss would be to lose myself while I
still continue to live.

X—X

ARKOPAUL DAS

Woke up, my eyes burning from the
smoke,
The exhaust was out, felt like I had a stroke,
Managed to crawl out, before it exploded in
my face,
Wish it would blow up, I'd be gone without
a trace.
We played around, she pulled the steering to
take a hard left,
By the time I had gained control, this truck
came to our aid,
I knew it went too far, I shouldn't have let
her;
Take the steering wheel cos now her body's
on the strecher.
People rushed in to put out the burning fire,
Windows smashed, doors charred, and it's
got a flat tire,
Red and blue lights flooded the area, yellow
tapes ran accross the street,
It was cordorned off as a crime scene, a
place where lovers are supposed to meet,
I ran around until I found the ambulance she
was in,
It's a miracle no one noticed the only

surviving victim.
By the time I reached, the ambulance had set
off before I could peak in,
I overheard someone speaking of where
she's being taken,
I sprinted all the way in the heat to the
hospital she was in,
My lungs giving out, sweat pouring down,
with onset of migraine,
Reached the place and asked around but no
one paid a heed,
I dart down the hallways until I found the
room that I need.
I felt like I was seeing a ghost when I saw
her,
She was hunched down over a body and her
eyes had a shower,
I peaked through the curtains to find white
clad men surrounding,
Ivs plugged in the arm, a stark beeping
noise, and a flat line on the screen.
When I finally realised who it was all I
wanted was to flee,
The distorted body on the bed wasn't her, it
was me.

ARKOPAUL DAS

X—X

EVEN GOD HAD TO DIE

I'm not cruel, I'm just a reflection of what
the world is,
You'd know how it is,
If you ever been kicked down on your
knees,
You're probably the one who did it,
And I don't hate you, here, let's sit,
Let's grab a cup of coffee and talk about
why we don't meet,
You'd grimace at the idea of me,
But forgiveness is actually so powerful,
You're just another human being is all I see.
I might dislike you, and I know I can be a
bitch,
I'm a human too, I don't always got shit in
my control,
But I don't lose touch with who I really am,
in my soul,
I don't really get influenced or violent,
But I do grow cold.
There was a time when I've been edgy and
immature,
And I've been running on a burning fuse for
sure,

But I never look back and regret, or wish I
had done things differently,
I'm also just a human and that's all I see.
And yes, I get very distant, even from
myself, and cold,
I believe life is like poker,
It's okay if you can't always call, it's okay if
you fold.
And let me just tell you one last thing before
I end,
You might wanna be in their life but end up
in their muse,
Things will always turn out the way it's
gonna, you can't ever choose,
And if you ever fight with me, and win,
you'll lose.

X—X

What am I supposed to do? With the kind
of past I had,
What am I supposed to do? Without going
mad.
What am I supposed to do? I can't relax.
So tell me what am I supposed to do?

I've been giving cold shoulders to my loved
ones,
They don't know the shit I go through.
Sometimes I wanna blow my head with a
gun,
Nail it to the wall probably with a screw.

Tell me what I'm supposed to do?
Where's that ray? The skies turned gray,
I'm screaming inside, but trying to
downplay,
No hope is there, none that's left,
I can see my future in the distance,
Fading away.
Turned the lights off, took my pills and sat
in the dark,
Maybe I will slowly fall asleep,
My anxiety kicks in, this life is bullshit,

And I'm so tired of climbing the ladder of
societal heirarch.

So tell me what I'm supposed to do?
This is nothing new.
Every word I wrote down, is something I've
said before.
I echo everything over and over,
My life's getting older but I'm not really
getting sober.
And it's over, I'm done,
I wish I could get out and see the sun, one
more time,
It's time, don't stop me, I've given so many
chances but had enough of it.

What was I supposed to do? Sit and cry?
What was I supposed to do? Say there's
something in my eye?
What was I supposed to do? I can't deny,
These thoughts been eating me up and I just
wanna die, yeah.

X—X

Now I'm cuddled in the sheets, with the
love of my life,
Dancing in the streets, with a beat up car we
both drive,
Cotton candy skies, with a ocean to dive,
Your love is beautiful like a park filled with
chives.

I've been feeling much better today, don't
know how long it will last,
I grind on and make it through, leaving
behind my past,
With a heavy heart I left everything behind,
I'm onto the become the next best thing,
better get in the line.

And girl you so fine, this love is divine,
I wish I could live a thousand lifetimes,
Just to call you mine,
And if death were to do us apart, it'd be such
a crime,
Because I'd choose you everytime, ten times
outa nine.

Time, that's what's been chasing me,

I hope I can be all the things I wanna be,
with you,
You make this forever come true,
And I didn't see this happening ever, it just
came out the blue.
It's all true, it's not a ruse, I'm your poetry,
you can be my muse,
I'm not that guy anymore, free for everyone
to use,
So I stopped fighting to prove myself and
called it a truce.

And it'd amuse, you,
When I tell you, my heart has been shattered
countless times,
I'm a sentence that doesn't end, a poem that
doesn't rhyme,
Which is a shame, cos I know I don't
deserve it,
And about time I give everything to people
who'd leave in a heartbeat.

But the shit times are over, I've grown older
and I'm sober,
It could be my intimidating personality, I

don't really know what drove her,
There's been so many people who stabbed
my back with a knife,
But fuck that cos
Now I'm cuddled in the sheets with the love
of my life.

X—X

Sometimes I have it right, sometimes I'm
somewhat loose,
I am not for everyone, it is for you to
choose.
I won't ever beg, ever again, even when on
my knees,
Because I've locked my heart away in a
freezer,
And threw away the keys.
Best believe me, I will get back up
everytime I fall,
Throw whatever you got at me,
I'll still hold my ground, I'll still stand tall.
Your efforts are futile, your bullets
richochets off my chest,
You think you're special but you're just like
the rest.
And I don't care for you, I am done putting
myself last,
This is that one time when the nice guy
came first.
If you heard rumours about me, just assume
they are true,
I don't have time to explain, or shit to prove.
I just do me, everyday, plain and simple,

EVEN GOD HAD TO DIE

Grind and do my best to get through
everyday,
Till my hair starts greying, till my temple
wrinkles.
Till my teeths give out, and my legs can't
take my weight no more,
Till my last breath, till there's fire left in my
core.
All my life I've been shown the door, they
told me I ain't worth shit,
I have no future, I'm toxic,
I'm a looser, a good for nothing, just sick, a
freak,
So here's to making through another year of
me being me,
And I ain't planning on leaving so quick.

X—X

ARKOPAUL DAS

So here I sit,
And as I write this, I look up at the sky,
because it is my only hope.
It's a starry night, dark, illuminated with
stars,
Just like fairy lights hanging in endless
cosmos,
Leo to the east, and betelgeuse shinning
bright in the west,
A cold wind whizzes past me, that familiar
chill,
The scent of incense sticks burning in the
distance,
And an appaling smell of burning crackers
hanging in the heavy air,
The city was celebrating, all lit up,
Yet here I am, drowning in darkness,
Reflecting on my thoughts, shivering yet
sweating,
A sense of growing restlessness inside me,
tormenting me,
The shivery winds and the stars unable to
calm my nerves,
For their is a storm, many in fact,
Hurricanes swirling and twirling deep

within my core,
Like a magma made of blood, crying out,
Trying to erupt out of every carve and
crevice of my body,
I feel trapped, in this body, in this life,
In this world, in this universe,
A prison, my soul confined within the binds
of the society,
For it wants to explore the eternal infinity,
But it can't.
So here I sit, and as I write this,
I look up at the sky because it is my only
hope.

X—X

I like that slow love, that innocent love,
The quick awkward glance over your
shoulder,
Followed by a smile, your cheeks pink,
That long gaze when the sun ray falls on
your eyelash,
When you sit on the beach and look at the
ocean,
Sipping on a lemonade, hand in hand with
me.
The way you shy away when your hand
grazes mine,
While we sit and chat in a library,
And nerd out on random bullshit that
doesn't make sense,
We get asked to be quiet and we giggle.
That love where you keep your hand on
mine,
Compare sizes and draw shapes in them,
While we chill in a park in one spring
afternoon,
Where the trees blossoms with flowers and
so does our love.
I like that forever love, no rush,
Waiting for an eternity just to be together,

Calm, patient, going to the ends of the
world,
Just make ends meet, just to make it work.
No looking back, no excuses, no getting
bored,
Just your eyes on one person, who becomes
your world,
You see the galaxies revolving in their
eyes,
The storm in their heart,
And you hug them tightly and hear the beat
getting faster,
Bodies and souls entwined, imperfections
surrendered,
And accept them for who they are.

X—X

Kids, let me unleash these venomous
beasts, lyrically ravaging you like vatican
priests,
I'm not a rapper, I write verses through a
poets mind,
But sometimes I go harder than Beaumont
and biggy combined.
Tell me about all the struggles you went
through as a child,
The world is my red carpet and I'm bout'a
walk down the aisle.
All the times you'd laugh at me when I was
down and weak,
Now you're as relevant to me as a floppy
disk.
My bars are handcrafted, like matt finish on
chrome,
It would make you cry even if you had dry
eye syndrome.
No brands on my body, I buried my pride
knee-deep,
My mind be exploding, I feel like I'm in the
Gaza strip.
I'm like Snowden, did the right thing, still a
traitor,

I keep my haters close, they my biggest
motivators.
They keep telling him, it's over, drop the
mic em,
But look at me, never touched the mic,
instead, I picked up the pen.
My rhymes go hard with trap beats or
pianola,
If I lived in Africa my bars would sound
sicker than Ebola.
I'm more important to myself than what
kindergarten was to froeble,
My words would hit you harder than them
bullets in Chernobyl.
You'll never outdo me or ever be the latest
vogue,
The only way you could get laid is if you
worked at a morgue.
I get it, I'm not famous, I'm insecure and
immature,
But you just an axe body spray tryna be
Christian Dior.
They say your poems are mainstream, and
your books are fogy,
But writing to me is what Amit shah is to

Modi.
I write poems, verses, and novels, I'm a
literary a la carte,
The only time I'll stop writing is when
death does us apart.

X—X

The darkness cleared out, and you were
dancing on the floor,
Tried to make my way to you but got stuck
at the door,
Trippy shinning lights whirled all around
above us,
People swaying around, but I was staring at
my crush.
You were wearing that red velvet deep cut
dress,
Do I look homeless or okay? I can't even
asses,
And this is feeling is not okay, I feel like I
should run away,
But you caught me staring at you and now
there was no gateway,
You raised your hand and called out to me,
You saw things me in me I couldn't see,
The music made me nervous, I could feel a
drop of sweat,
Which song was playing? Oh, it's Lord
Huron's "The night we met".
You stretched out your hand as I met it with
mine,
Grabbed you by the waist, fingers

entwined,
If love is illegal then I'm about to commit a
crime,
You are my poetry and I am just a verse
that doesn't rhyme.
We tapped our feet and swayed to the slow
lofi music,
You will find love in the strangest people,
especially in the ones you don't seek,
The way she looked and smiled at me had
me going weak,
I don't know how we vibed so hard cos I'm
such a geek.
And slowly the darkness resumed, and
everyone started to disappear,
My mind started to feel conflicted,
surprised to even see her here,
Slowly I rose up as you turned into dust in
front of me,
My head felt messy, I thought I'm going
crazy,
I swear I felt what Andrew felt when he lost
his Gwen Stacy.

X—X

I've lost so many guy friends just because I can't fucking stand the way they talk about women among themselves.

The derogatory terms or the mentality, I don't know which one is the worse of it. It's not even that they are too horny or just wanna get laid, and it's not even the objectification or seeing them as playthings, because it goes way deeper than that; something profoundly flawed in their psyche because trust me, the vivid, graphic and honestly sickening descriptions of what they would do to a woman that I've heard, just, just leaves me absolutely speechless.

It's arbitrarily disgusting how they see women in general, in a carnal sadistic way, as a means to obtain nonconsensual perverted pleasure and then jettison their existence out the window and move on to the next possible prey, the moment they had had enough. A conventional excuse is a fact that in the past some girl probably did them wrong or broke their heart, but take it from someone whose heart has been ripped apart numerous times, and whose self-esteem and dignity has been dragged through the mud; let me tell you my outlook on women haven't changed one bit, I have nothing but the utmost respect for women. Men and women alike. People in general. People who deserve respect to be precise.

You don't have to respect someone who is genuinely a horrible person, who manipulated you and did you wrong. Block them, cut them off, obliterate the feelings you have from your heart slowly, do whatever you need to find peace. Sure, hurtful words can be exchanged in an argument or in a relationship on the brink of getting toxic, it's understandable, happens to the best of us. And no, I'm not gonna sit there and preach pretending to be a saint, I've let my emotions get the better off me, I've cussed people out, said stupid shit and it's okay because I've learned from it. Hate them for a month, two months, three, then move along with your life. But changing your psychology entirely and becoming irreverent towards a whole gender altogether does not make you cool, it just means you haven't been brought upright, it just means you are a monster.

Some men might argue that but in the 21st-century women are the same and that they have all the privileges in the world and opportunities to ruin a man, I've heard this argument countless times. And fine, I agree to an extent, I'm sure there are some awful women out there who are up to no good, fuck, I've personally come across many. Firstly equality and male/female privileges is a different topic altogether and secondly reverting back to this topic, I'm gonna have to be real with you chief, in my experience, the aforementioned brutal and perverted mentality of looking at the opposite gender as means to garner sexual pleasure is far more prevalent in men than in women.

You cannot rationalize being a detestable person and holding a grudge or a macabre perspective on women. It's simply repulsive and disgusting and it needs to stop. Respect and generosity are a must; never linger at a table where it's not being served.

X—X

I sit in this room, the walls are closing in,
Blood is trickling down from the ceiling,
I wish I could scream,
But an unseen force has got to my throat,
Choking me,
I cough out,
And all I see is fog around me.
The mist clears, and you appear,
A silhouette of what used to be my
universe,
All the galaxies, swirling in your eyes,
I was hypnotized.
I couldn't fathom, how to deal with this
loss,
The claustrophobia crept in, I was sweating,
My back was plastered against the wall,
Pushing me onward to the opposite end.
Towards you.
There's no escape from this darkness and
agony,
No windows, or a door, nowhere I could
escape,
This was meant to be. I was destined for
this.
Stuck in an infinite loop of time and

pressure,
In this vast cosmos,
Crushing me into dust, just to do it again,
And again,
There's no escape.
With a heavy heart, I get back up,
The fog makes me blind, my mind blurry,
I could barely make out the distant mirages
of my old self,
Like I was looking at a mirror,
A mirror that showed me what I could
never experience,
What I could never leave,
For I am stuck in this infinite loop of time,
With these four walls, and the darkness.

x—x

This was the day I knew I was gonna do
it,
The sheer agony got to me and I was ready
to slit open my wrists,
Came back from the school and tossed my
bag,
Crashed on the bed, my head felt like it was
getting snagged,
The minimal distraction was over, darkness
swallowed me instantly,
Life played before my eyes, memories I
would have liked to forget immediately,
Nothing good ever came out of this and
suddenly it was three hours,
10 on the clock sharp I got up, even when I
wanted to cower,
My mind was vacant and I was numb to my
feet,
It was like I was possessed with a demon I
couldn't defeat,
I felt through my study table, cos basically I
was blind,
Didn't turn on the light, cos that might have
changed my mind,
I had done research before on how to do it

so I know,
There used to be a knife in the drawers,
where the fuck did it go,
I briskly shuffled through, getting chills
down my spine,
Found some asthma pills and also a packet
of nine;
Sleeping pills, Xanax would have probably
worked better but they don't give that out
here without prescription,
So I had to go for what I had and make a
quick decision,
I dropped them in my palm and put them in
my mouth,
I stared at my silhouette in the mirror with a
tiny shrink of doubt,
Was on the verge of tears but I couldn't
even cry,
Should have used water but I swallowed
them dry.
Sat back down on the bed waiting for it to
hit me,
Nothing happened for a bit until my head
got all wobbly,
In quick succession I fell down and

managed to trash my body on the bed,
I fought hard to keep my eyes open but wait
I wanted to be dead,
My life didn't flash before my eyes, it was
basically like I was drowning,
My mind was blank and I didn't know what
was happening,
Paranoia kicked in and my heartbeat got
quicker,
This isn't supposed to be it, the last light
flickered;
Off, and I don't know what happened, I
probably blacked out;
Or fainted, but life called for a time-out,
I jolted awake and could not really think,
I felt sick to my stomach and had to rush to
the sink,
Barely managed to get there before I threw
up all the pills,
Collapsed to the floor while my head did a
backward wheel,
Woke up a few hours later, sick, with a
shitty headache,
Like a hangover, but with carnage at my
rake,

Washed my face off and slapped myself
hard,
Came back to reality cos that's what the
moment required,
Took one last look at the ghastly face and
the circles that had blackened,
Went back to school for my daily dose of
distraction like nothing ever happened,
Managed to get through the day as usual,
somehow,
Little did I know this self harm bullshit
would be like a daily thing now.

X—X

EVEN GOD HAD TO DIE

I've been down this road before,
The junction in life where the road
diverges,
And I don't know which one to choose
Because both are filled with an equal
amount of sadness
And misery.
It never works out, it only kills you more,
And all I'm trying is to fix the mess,
The mess I've become for the people,
Who messed me up,
The people who did me wrong and left me
in the cold,
The life that taught me that I'm alone,
And hit me with its worst, and asked me to
stand up,
And stay strong.
And for once I didn't want to stay strong
I wanted to break down and sob and cry and
weep,
And expected someone to hold me and tell
me,
That it will be fine,
But here comes the reality check, I'm alone,
And this is how it has always been,

This is how it will always be,
Surviving and healing and trying my best,
Giving my everything and getting the bare
minimum back,
But I shall keep grinding, soldering on to
the unknown,
This is not the path I would choose,
But then again,
At this point in my life,
What do I have left to lose?

EVEN GOD HAD TO DIE

She will leave me hanging just like she
always does,
But I'm a fool, and I'm mad in love,
She will be texting everyone except for me,
I'll be here by my phone expecting a text for
me.
What is this phase? I don't know what to call
it,
Where we talk for hours but ignore each
other at the college,
I just want you to acknowledge,
The feelings that you have for me?
Oh wait, maybe you don't? Maybe you just
be playing me.
Leading me on, making me dream of things
I wish we could be,
You tell me that you love me but then you
start ghosting me,
You'd ghost me for weeks and pop up like
nothing even happened,
I see your love fading damn this is such a
sad end-ing,
Of all the things that I'd imagined,
You got too many priorities and I'm at a
tight end.

Just when I feel like I'll move on, you'll get
all mushy and nice,
Make me melt just for the moment and later
I pay the price,
The inconsistency kills me and my friends
say I deserve better,
They tell me you don't care, they tell me
"Forget her",
Maybe they are right, maybe I should listen
to them,
Cos you make all this promises and still act
the same,
I'll finally be over you then my phone will
be ringing,
It will be you on the other side, again,
leaving me hanging,
I don't wanna pick it up, but it's so hard for
me to stop,
Cos I'm a fool, and I'm mad in love.

X—X

You can call me when all the lights go
out,
But I can't reply now, cos my head is filled
with doubts,
You can't hear me even when I'm crying out,
Screaming till I can't cos that's what life's
been about.
These tears will make me choke and this
darkness will swallow me,
I wish I was blind cos there's so much shit
that I have to see,
With one leg hanging off the edge, I was
grasping on for my life,
I still wasn't sure if I should pull back or
take the fucking dive;
Into the abyss of the dead, carrying all the
debts I didn't pay,
I embraced myself to get pierced with all
things left unsaid,
Fissures in my heart, that's from where I had
bled,
I thought my time has come but I was
terribly misled.
You could call me when it's all said and
done,

If I'm not hurting for you then it's not really
fun,
You could see that I've always been on the
run,
If I haven't cut you off yet then just wait for
your turn.
With a nod and a smile so many people I
have fooled,
Got away from bs they threw at me and the
shit they tried to pull.
Battered and bruised, I put them in my
muse,
Blood dripping from my arm from all the
times that I got used.
In the end I went down fighting but I
received a fatal blow,
I felt my mind go numb and my heartbeat
started to slow.
I pulled the noose tighter and hung there
from the rope,
I had lost so many people but now I had lost
hope.

x—x

EVEN GOD HAD TO DIE

You took me to the edge, and said "This
is the end of the world"
"What do you mean?" I asked,
You pointed at the stars and told me you'd
call,
Maybe I was too dumb to believe that I
wouldn't fall,
My mind was taken away already with the
scent of ethanol. "I believe in you" you said
without a doubt,
You took my hand and laid it out,
The plans of our future, I could hear it nice
and loud,
You smiled and whispered "You did so
much, I'm so proud"
I said that I was nothing, the breeze flew by
us,
The sea gurgled the words unspoken and the
words we should discuss.
Your eyes glittered with the lingering aura
of that love song,
Your hands grazed the back of my neck and
we swayed along,
To the wind, as the lights slowly went out in
the distance,

The city slept but these two hearts were
quite resistant.
You drank the last drop of jack and grinned
in bliss,
Drunk in love', you planted a kiss, on my
lips,
I could taste those fish and the chips,
From earlier when we just had our date,
It was like Chernobyl, radioactive felicity hit
me like those bullets,
But I was unaware of the oncoming eclipse.
Was trying not to be cliche but I ended up
saying that,
You took my sorrow, took my pain, "I think
we should head back" you said, cos it had
started to rain,
I walked you back to your place, and we
kissed again,
It was hard loving you so much and still
staying sane.
I would wait for you for the weeks to come,
You didn't exist for people, dead to some,
No words, no letters, not a sign of your
scent,

EVEN GOD HAD TO DIE

I didn't realize when you said end of the
world, this is what you meant.

x—x

I fall in love with the thought of flying
away,
With the conversations I hear among
complete strangers,
Until they walk away from me, until they
are nothing but a small dot of blackness in
the distance,
Under a red afternoon sky.
I liked watching birds flying away up above
me,
Plane disappear in the clouds,
It filled me with a happy but a melancholic
aura of wanderlust,
Of chasing what I don't have, of discovering,
Of flying high and see the buildings grow,
Smaller, and smaller,
And smaller,
Of being amongst the clouds where I don't
have to look up to see the sun,
Where I won't have to see people turn
around a corner and disappear,
Cos now we are all in the same boat,
suspended in the air,
Defying the gravity,
Carrying all sorts of happy and sad stories

within us,
Life leading us to the same destination but
for different reasons.
Don't you get so immersed in the stories of
people around you?
Don't you feel the eerie quietness and the
vibration in a plane,
And a bustle in the background, thoughts
crisscrossing our minds,
In a rhythmic, astral manner, at the same
time.
That guy who's going for a job interview
that he isn't gonna get,
Or that tall man fighting for leg room in the
economy class of SpiceJet,
Or how about those long lost lovers who
haven't met,
Our lives are really so interconnected but we
don't know that, yet.
I look down and find the ocean and the
greenery and the clouds and the cities spread
out,
And I realise once upon a time I was down
there looking up
At a similar machine filled with stories,

Flying away from me and disappearing in
the endless atmosphere,
And I still feel just as happy and
melancholic cruising towards a change,
Just as I used to feel as child down there.
That night when my head hit the pillow,
I realized,
We all wanna fly, but when we do, we start
missing the ground below.

How can I ever love somebody if I never
love me?
You're feeling empty and alone, cos you see,
You've been told you aren't enough,
You have been told your nose is a bit
crooked,
Your forehead is big and your body
shouldn't be seen naked,
Your jawline is a bit bent and your tits are
non existent,
So you live with the fact that you aren't
worth it,
That no one will ever love you for shit,
Because the society needs you to buy the
shit it sells,
The lies, the bullshit, the make up, the
clothes,
Lol swell,
The self doubt it puts in your head,
Turning yourself into the very thing you
wished, was dead,
Telling you, you aren't enough,
Through the people, the media, it's all a
sham and a bluff,
So I turn to the mirror every morning and I'll

tell you what I see,
The person that looks back at me is enough
for me.
Everytime I walk into a room, my
confidence is the key,
Everytime I walk into a relationship,
I know I am capable of giving the love I
give to me,
Cos I know,
How can I ever love somebody if I never
love me?

X—X

Distant lights flicker in the distance, as I
stand here,
On the ledge, carrying the weight of the
world,
My mind is groggy, my pupils dilated, my
head swaying,
With the wind.
Tears flow down my eyes, as I reflect on
my battered and bruised body,
My childhood, or the lack of one,
The abuse and torture of the world,
Beating me down until I had nothing left,
Just an empty, hollow, sorry excuse of a
physical entity,
Which can disappear and no one would
even notice.
I wanted to escape from the past, I needed
to.
And the abyss way down there looked so
inviting.
Nothing flashed before my eyes, except for
the distant city lights,
No memories, no more erupting traumas,
No more depression and anxiety of future.
A chilly gust of wind whizzes past me as I

glance down,
And my head turns.
I've always been afraid of heights, but not
anymore.
I don't care anymore about my vertigo. Of
nothing really.
A quarter of my feet is hanging off the
edge,
My calves tremble, and my body shivers,
The ground down there is calling out to me.
I close my eyes, and remember the times
people told me it gets better,
Told me to pray to God, that he will fix
everything.
I lean forward, my weight giving in to the
gravity,
And the weight of simply existing is lifted.
Air blows past me in a state of freefall.
I open my eyes one more time to look at the
sky and the stars,
Freeing myself of all the torment and
sickness,
And I tell myself if he does exist
somewhere,

God should be the one begging for my forgiveness.

"I realy wanted my last year to be my last year. But I am still around, trying to knock it away."

\-   Pete Davidson.

Arkopaul Das is a self-published writer, streamer, youtuber, poet, blogger, trader and a self-proclaimed cinephile. He loves all things aesthetic and considers himself to have a creative mind. His other books consist of the infamous "Insomniac" and "Sociopath: Deceitful Game" and his non-fiction self-help book "You need to hear this shit."

www.ingramcontent.com/pod-product-compliance
Lightning Source LLC
Chambersburg PA
CBHW061527120726
48001CB00004B/1425